Treewalker's Gift

Overcoming the Fear of Being Loved

This book is dedicated to the individuals in my life who saw something special in me that I could not see.   To the small group of women who held me up with their prayers, support and constant encouragement as I struggled to share my truth in the book, I am so grateful.

To the family I have gathered along my path of life and woven into my heart, I thank you for standing with me through the fears that crowded my life on many occasions.   I could not have gone on without you.

I want to acknowledge Susanna Steeg who gave me the encouragement to start this book and met often with me to help keep it on track.   Her gentle guidance and humble spirit as she edited each page reminded me often of God's love for me.

I dedicate this book to all that have felt the brokenness that shame, fear and neglect bring to one's life. May you discover your own path to freedom and truth and live above the pain.

To the Tree who will always live in my heart: 55555555 "I will never forget you"

Chapter 1

Grandfather Browndeer

I was six years old the year my parents dropped me off in the woods where my grandfather lived.

I had never met my grandfather, only overheard my parents say he lived in a small remote cabin in the woods of Missouri. My father spoke of him only once when sharing how when he was eight years old, he had run away from home because he hated the Native lifestyle and the quietness of the woods. He rejected the words his father spoke to him about the Great Spirit.

My father did not want to be associated with his heritage and hated being called "Redskin" or "Indian." I was only four years old the first time I saw him savagely beat a young man because he referred to my father as a lazy, drunk Indian. Watching as my father's fists struck that young man; seeing the blood stream from his face put a deep fear in my heart of what my father might possibly do to me if I ever said anything bad about him. I worried constantly about upsetting him and would not allow myself to fall asleep unless I knew he was sleeping or passed out from drinking too much.

I grew up that day. I replaced the innocence of playful adventures and hopeful dreams of being loved with fears of sudden attacks and family violence. With every punch to that young man's face, I knew that being a child was dangerous and held certain pain.

From that day forward, I began to learn how to stay alive by avoiding my feelings, guarding my words and never allowing my desires or needs to be known in my family. If I could be good at this, I would be safe. I learned to stand guard in the most invisible way possible. I was always one word or action away from feeling the same pain and disgrace that I had seen on that boy's face. Every day

I woke up uncertain if I would be alive to go to sleep that night. I came to hope more for death than the agony of facing another day with the monster that grew stronger every day within my home. I kept myself alive by thinking of how I could protect my mother and little brother. They were my father's targets for abuse if I did not intervene. I felt myself disappear a little more every time my father hit me or yelled at me or violated me. I was always waiting for someone to open the door to safety and caring that I pounded on with all my strength, but no one came and I grew to know that no one would.

Even as a small child, I had very little that gave me hope or any desire to live. The driving force for everything I did was that my mother would someday accept and love me. I believed that every time my body felt pain from my father's angry fists, it would mean one less time my little brother or mother would feel the same. This token of my love kept my fatal hope alive. I was certain that if I could do this enough that my mother might see my worth and want me around. This became the purpose of my life. Someday, someone would see something special in me and want to love me.

As a teen, my father made his way across the country staying short periods of time in people's homes doing chores for room and board and then moving on. He was a gypsy in many ways, for he could charm people with his words and knew how to get them to give him what he wanted before he moved on. He often said the road was his friend and he had no desire to part from it. He moved my family so many times that I lost count. Many of the moves resulted from us being migrant workers during various picking seasons. When we finished picking the field of a farmer we would have to move to find another. We put everything in the trunk of the Studebaker and my father would start driving. In the off seasons, my father sometimes rented a small house for us but that only lasted a short time before the owner of the house came and threw us out because my father had gotten drunk and put in jail and we could not pay the rent.

Sometimes the police came with the welfare office and took us from our home. I hated leaving my mother because I did not trust that I would ever see her again. On those occasions when my sister and I and my younger brother were taken out of the home, my mother would stand out in the streets and scream as loud as she could, causing all the neighbors to come out to see what was going on. I was always so embarrassed and tried to stay hidden from the disparaging looks shot at my family. My mother wore a housecoat and bathrobe all the time. She had short coal black hair that was void of any curl and her lips were sunk in because she did not have any teeth left and could not afford any store-bought ones. I remember looking back at her from the rear seat of the state car with tears in my eyes and two very conflicting feelings in my heart, Sorrow and Relief.

We never stayed long in the homes of the people the welfare office called foster parents, and I suspect it was because my father was so convincing with his words. He would tell the welfare people that I liked to cause trouble for him and was always lying about being beaten. He told them I was a very clumsy child and wasn't right in the head. If anyone asked me if that was true, all I could think about was how my father had beaten that young man. I did not want that to happen to me, so I told my father's truth. I could never talk about my father's drinking or the violence that came with it. When the welfare office took me home, I was always punished for letting someone see a bruise or a welt. The story was always that we were in an accident or fell down. When my parents had to come to a meeting or school conference, I had to say that he was sick or out of town or working. My mother did not drive and wasn't allowed to go anywhere without my father, anyway. She told us to do what he said and there was no further discussion. I always had to guess about what the truth should be when it came to my parents. No one from the welfare office ever checked on us because we were always moving and never in one place long enough for people to become suspicious or look beyond my father's words and deceptive smile.

I only remember one time someone offered to help me. A woman spotted me at the creek near our home trying to wash the blood dripping from my face. I could not get it to stop no matter how hard I pressed my hand against my forehead. When she could not find my parents, she took me to the emergency room to get stitches. When the doctor asked how it happened, I slipped up and told the truth that my father had thrown a beer bottle across the room and hit me in the head because I dropped my spoon on the floor. The police took my father to the police station and when I got home, my mother was really mad at me. I remember how she was crying and screaming that I had hurt her because the police took my father away and it was all my fault. She grabbed my arm and threw me into a tiny hall closet. She screamed that if I ever said anything bad against my father again she would never want to be around me. I had to be better, I knew that I had been selfish and spoke words that I was told not to. I had caused my mother's pain and did not know how to help her. My tears started to flow down my face but my mother said that I had nothing to cry about. I was the one who hurt our family and brought shame on my father. I just wanted to make my mother feel better.

I was in that closet a long time trying to hold back tears and not move so that my mother would not come and scream at me. When the door finally opened, she yanked me out and made me walk down to the police station with her to tell them that I had lied about what had happened; my father never hurt me. Lying became my truth when it came to anything about my family and who I was.

Hiding the truth from outsiders was our family's number one goal. We did this to protect our family and make sure that no one came in and took us away.

The police believed me and released my father that night. I was beaten very badly after we got home. I knew that it was going to happen because of how he gripped my hand so tightly the whole way home, not allowing me to break loose and run away. The blows hit hard but it did not hurt as much as remembering my mother's words of how she would leave me if I ever spoke badly against my father or shared what happened in our family again. That night, I made a promise to my mother that I would never talk about any of the bad things that happened in our family again. And I promised myself that I would never let anyone see my hurts again, no matter how much pain I was in.

The only way I knew to keep those promises was to shut down my hope for love and caring. I accepted that lies would protect my family; this became my whole reality. I spent so much time trying to figure out what I should say to people when they asked what happened to me, that I finally stopped talking and avoided any questions. I told myself if I did not say anything or tell anyone, that it just didn't happen. I became very skilled at covering up not only my bruises and cuts, but also the internal scars of fears that grew deep inside of me. Pain within my family was creating a callous on my heart that grew thicker and deeper with each cruel act. I was slowly burying any hope of being loved and living a life without pain or shame.

When I heard about going to stay with my grandfather, I worried he would be like my father. I did not want to be with him if that was true but no one asked me if I wanted to go, just like I had never been asked about what I wanted in the past. I just did as I was told and hoped I could find a safe place to hide there.

I would not have known they were dropping me off in the woods of my grandfather if I had not overheard my parents talking about going on a trip across country in the car with my older sister and little brother and not wanting me to go with them. The last time they left on a trip and did not take me, the people across the road called the police and the welfare office came and put me in a home with lots of other children until my parents returned. Since my parents did not want the police involved again, my grandfather's

woods seemed best because no one would find me there. It was on

the way to New York where my mother's family lived and they were

going to spend the summer. I thought to myself that it was a strange

thing for them to say no one would find me there, because who

would even want to look for me?

I wondered if Grandfather wanted me to come. Did he even

know that I was coming? We did not have a phone and my parents

would not have sent a letter since they did not know how to read or

write. My only comfort with the thought of being in the woods was

that my father would not be around. I looked forward to being

surrounded by trees and the creatures that roamed in and around

them.

The trip to reach my grandfather's woods was a long one, for

we had to travel by car from Oregon to Missouri. My father had

decided to drive straight through; we did not stop to sleep or eat.

My mother brought a loaf of bread, a jar of mayonnaise, and a

package of bologna to make sandwiches as we drove. We choked

them down without anything to drink because my father did not want us to need to stop to go to the bathroom. He was always in a hurry and did not want anyone to inconvenience him in any way.

I dozed off and on in the backseat but woke often to the sharp, bitter words of my father's cursing at my mother and anyone on the road who got in his way. I felt a strange sense of comfort come over me as I thought of the woods and the silence I had come to know when I had spent time climbing trees. I hated feeling scared all the time and hearing the violence and rejection that came from my parents. My body was always tense, shoulders held tight. I had to be on guard, ready to run and escape the attacks of my father. Riding in the car for such a long time frightened me because there was nowhere to escape to, nowhere to hide. I scrunched my body down into a ball on the floor behind the passenger's seat, the safest place to avoid my father's unpredictable fists when my eyes were too heavy to stay awake.

My older sister did not know my father's wrath and I had wondered how this could be. I was often told that she was beautiful and witty and knew how to please my father. She hated having me around and I knew that if I got into her things or said anything to upset her, my father would come after me. I stayed away from her and always walked several blocks behind her when we came home from school. Her eyes cut through me and when she was talking to her many friends, she would turn to them and say something and they would laugh as they looked my direction. I did not know how to be like my sister but I often wanted to find a way. I tried so hard to not do anything to upset my parents, hoping that would protect me, but I was never good enough. The more ridicule and pain I felt, the more I would try harder to earn a place in their hearts. I knew I would never be important to them, but I just could not stop trying. I learned how to escape the pain of this reality by creating others in my mind that took the pain for me. "Never good enough" was the tune that always played in my head. This was my theme song, my go to music that haunted me and drove me further into prisons of rejection and fear.

Late in the morning of a cold summer day, my parents put me out into my grandfather's woods. I stood looking around me as the old tan Studebaker drove off in a cloud of black smoke. I did not know which way to walk. My eyes filled with tears and my tiny body shivered in the shadows of the tall oak trees. I was cold in my short-sleeved grey dress that had a torn pocket on one side from stuffing too many rocks into it and a bulging pocket on the other side from the half eaten bologna sandwich that I saved in case I was hungry later. My tiny frame made it easy to hide behind the trunks of trees, a skill that had protected me on several occasions.

My hair was thick and tangled, with natural curls that felt heavy on my shoulders. My eyes were void of color and light, or so I thought on the few times I had ventured to look in a mirror. I was always afraid to see what I looked like because my family had told me so often how ashamed they were to have such an ugly child. I spent many hours hidden away in locked places because they feared people knowing that I was a part of their family. I was constantly afraid that someone would see me and be so horrified that they would turn away and run if they ever looked directly at me. My father's words rang loudly in my ears, becoming the only mirror of who I was and what others saw when they looked at me.

A stream of sunlight touched my shoulder and I realized how cold I was. It felt warm and safe to stand in the warmth of the sunlight; it calmed my shivering so that I could feel my breath again within me. My thoughts had been racing on so many fearful, shame-filled tracks about my life that I needed the intensity of the sun's rays to steady me and bring me back into the present. When the clouds slowly drifted over and I felt a chill, I walked further into the sunlight in whatever direction it led. I was not looking for grandfather, as I could not trust that he really even existed. I only wanted to be warm and find a safe place to rest.

I was familiar with being alone, with trying to find shelter and warmth when angry words and shouting started in my home. I usually chose tall grasses, trees, or large cement pipes to hide and spend the night until things calmed down. No one came looking for me and I found comfort resting somewhere that no one knew where I was. I had traded my desire for being cared about for the peacefulness of silence and hiding.

From the corner of my eye, I spotted a deer standing alone near an opening in the woods and when it saw me, it did not run away. It merely looked at me; its beautiful dark eyes and brown skin drew me closer. When I came close to the place he was nibbling at the grass, he slowly began walking away and I followed along at a distance. I stopped when he stopped, and took small bites on my sandwich when he indulged in the lush grass on the sides of the narrow, faint path he chose. His casual stride said he had travelled this path often and knew just where the tastiest grass grew. After a while, the trees thinned out and the patches of grass grew larger and there was a wide opening ahead that the deer ran toward. I ran as fast as I could to catch up to him, but came to a complete stop as I caught a glimpse of what was in the clearing.

In front of me was a small wooden shack of a cabin, swallowing the sunshine. The logs were gray and worn and there was a small stack of rocks piled on the roof for a chimney. The deer was now nowhere in sight and I looked frantically for him, not wanting to be alone. A brown skinned man with gray hair appeared from the shaded side of the cabin with a blanket over his shoulder. He looked at me without alarm as I stood at the edge of his home. His eyes were dark and held my glance just as the deer had done. I felt no fear, no need to run or hide. I waited, not knowing what I should do without fear to direct me.

The man motioned for me to come closer and as I slowly approached, he sat down on the ground and held the blanket out to me. The door to the cabin was open and he again motioned with his hand for me to go in. My feet walked toward him and I stood looking at his eyes. They were familiar, but the emotion I felt when I looked in them was not. I was not afraid; I did not feel ashamed. Something stirred deep inside my belly and whispered a word I had never known....safe.

"Grandfather?"

"Yes, child, I have been preparing," his gravelly voice was gentle.

"How did you know I was coming?" I asked him.

"My heart knew, and I listened and did as it told me."

I took the blanket from his outstretched hand and walked into the cabin where I saw two mats lying on the dirt floor, one near the door and the other by a pile of rocks blackened by fire. I quickly put the blanket down on the mat nearest the door and walked out to Grandfather. We did not talk, but I followed him at a distance as he moved about gathering branches and placing them in a pile just outside the cabin.

"Are you hungry, child?"

My bologna sandwich was long gone and my stomach made hungry noises but I did not want to burden my grandfather or take his food.

"No, Grandfather," I blurted quickly.

His eyes held my gaze until something inside of me forced my eyes down and I felt tears on my hot cheeks.

"Where did those words come from, Little One?" His voice was not accusatory, just curious.

I did not know what to say to him, but finally answered, "My mouth, Grandfather."

"No child, you spoke your fear from a dark place. What is your truth?"

Truth? I wasn't sure if I knew what truth was. Was it something that made others happy? Was it keeping the bad secrets and saying what I was told to say? Was it making sure no one would see my fear?

Grandfather interrupted my wild thoughts, "Child, did your heart speak, or did your head speak from fear?"

I took a long time to answer before I said, "My head, Grandfather."

He spoke quietly but firmly in a way that made me want to lean in and listen: "I ask only one thing from you while you are with me, Child, and that is to always speak from the truth of your heart. And I will do the same with you."

I did not know how to speak from my heart. I only knew how to speak from my fears around violence, shame and total isolation. "I will try, Grandfather, but my heart has never been allowed to speak,"

"I will teach your heart how to speak, and it will whisper its fears to me and shout its joy like the red sky over the mountains in the morning and the abundance of stars at night." Grandfather's voice held the conviction I did not feel.

I felt my heart grow sad inside me. Grandfather was painting a picture that I longed to hold inside, but I knew I would never have it as my own. I could never speak my truth because it would only bring me punishment. My heart did not know how to freely let go of what I held inside; I always had to think of how my words could harm me. Joy and freedom to speak the truth would never happen for me. He did not know who I truly was and how bad I was on the inside. I stood silent trying to keep my tears from falling down my cheeks. I didn't want him to see them and send me away.

Grandfather walked to a basket by the cabin and handed me a root plant, wiping it vigorously against his pants. I took a bite; it had a bitter taste that made my nose and eyes scrunch together.

"Do you not like it, Child?"

"It's okay, Grandfather," the words came out before I could stop them. I felt his eyes look at me again and I knew my heart had not spoken its truth. He waited until I found courage to say, "No, Grandfather, I don't like it."

He nodded his head in approval and took the root from my hands. He went inside the cabin and brought out a leftover biscuit from his morning meal. "This will taste better. Your heart has spoken truth and it has brought you reward."

Truth. Reward. Safe. Grandfather's words were strange and I was not certain how to respond, so I simply nodded and quietly sat on the ground to eat the biscuit he had given me, allowing all the unspoken things about the day to settle in my mind.

The summer days were hot and the nights warm. Grandfather and I fell into a rhythm of living together. He did his thing and I did mine. But he did not ignore me. I had a sense that he knew where I was all the time, even when we were not together.

I ran through the meadows and climbed every tree I could find. I hid in the tall grasses and picked flowers and listened to the sound the meadow-grasses made as the wind played through them. I turned as brown as berry and sniffed the sunshiny breeze from high up in the treetops. Grandfather called me Treewalker because I was always climbing every tree my eyes landed on.

"Treewalker," he would say in his quiet, velvety voice, "what do you hear?"

On this day, he had directed me out to the middle of a bubbling creek, where I perched on a rock with the waters flowing around me on either side.

"I hear the water, Grandfather."

"No, close your eyes and tell me what you hear. Your eyes are getting in the way of your ears."

"OK," I said. I scrunched my eyes closed and concentrated. "A bird?"

"What's the bird saying, Treewalker?"

"I don't know, Grandfather."

"Keep your eyes closed and listen."

"It's saying 'tweet!'"

Grandfather's voice had an edge of laughter to it, even though he spoke with more force, "No, child, now close your eyes, close your ears.

Listen to the bird and feel it. What is the bird saying?"

Ohhhh. "The bird likes to fly, Grandfather."

"Hmmm. Good. Your heart has spoken to you, because you did not let its truth get lost in what you saw and heard. Treewalker, your heart will know many things if you allow the Great Spirit to live there and guide you. You will see the hearts of others as you release the pain of your life and breathe deeply of the Great Spirit's guidance. Then you will understand that what you see and hear won't destroy you. Carrying words spoken in anger and not of truth can weigh your heart down, but the words of the Great Spirit sets you free to release the heaviness you carry and allow you to see the truth of your life. Do not allow your eyes and ears to trap you into believing lies and passing them on as truth to your heart. You spoke correctly when you said the bird loves to fly. The bird takes in all that is around it and then carefully choses where to sit down and take its rest. Your heart can do the same, Treewalker, if you choose to fly above the words that overtake you and find your place to sit in peace and truth."

I wondered if these were the words my father did not like to hear and if the bitterness of his heart came from not resting in the truth, I could not imagine my father ever being in this place, in this peace, in this gentle way of living. I did not believe that my father had ever accepted the ways of the Great Spirit, but had made his mission to destroy the words of Grandfather and do battle with the Great Spirit. There was much for my mind to think on, but I felt a peacefulness pass over me like the rushing waters of the stream that flowed beside the rock on which I was perched. I did not want this peace to ever leave me. I wanted to keep myself on the rock, with my grandfather, listening with my heart to the bird that spoke of freedom of flight towards the Truth.

I slept outside on those warm summer nights, curled up in the meadow. I didn't need any blankets. Grandfather showed me how to shape the tall grass into a bed—a bed so comfortable that it felt like someone was holding me all night long. The meadow was so safe. I slept better there than I had in my whole life. Deer walked by, like a whisper, always respectful. They never bothered me and I wasn't afraid, even when a curious doe nuzzled my cheek one morning as the sun was coming up.

During that summer with Grandfather, he taught me that my eyes and ears were just doorways to something deeper. He showed me how the feel of the wind on my cheek was actually a kiss. I came to know the warmth of the sunshine as one of my first and best hugs. As our days whiled away, he showed me how to cook squirrel and bake biscuits. He never measured anything. I watched everything and learned.

"What do you feel today, Treewalker?" Grandfather and I were sitting in the meadow, with the grass curled up around us. We were making baskets from the long blades that were now turning brown from the hot summer days.

"I feel the softness of the lap I'm sitting in, Grandfather. I feel the whispers of sweet words from the birds and the passing breeze tickling my ears and stirring up laughter inside of me. I feel warm hugs from the sun and the promise from the creek that I will have its refreshing cool touch soon."

"Treewalker, you are learning to listen and see from your heart."

"I have learned from you, Grandfather,"

"No, Child, I only helped you close your eyes of fear. The Great Spirit has come to your heart and set you free to see and hear the words of truth. I will not always be with you, but He will and He will help you find the truth when the lies grow strong around you. Don't let anyone rob you of the truth that comes from the Great Spirit. Learn how to close your eyes and sit in His lap and hear His whispers of care for you."

I laid my head back and looked up at the passing clouds and realized I was happy....really happy. I was with someone who wanted to be with me. I was safe and there were no angry words or violence. I felt at home in this meadow, with this man who spoke little but said so much to my heart. "Grandfather, I will sit in this lap and remember as long as I can."

"May your heart remember long after your mind has forgotten, Treewalker."

Chapter 2

Meadow Memories

I loved being in the meadow at the center of my Grandfather's woods. The tall soft grass I felt when I reached the meadow's edge greeted me with little white daisies that grew abundantly and brushed against my bare legs. I walked along the fresh paths deer made on their way to the stream, excited to see what the night had left for me. I could always breathe deeply here of the gentle freshness of grass; I loved rolling in the tall blades that hid me from the view of others' eyes. Grandfather was teaching me so much about living in the woods and finding laughter to replace my tears.

Our early morning walks through the meadows always held lessons for me, and today was no different. My eyes landed on something sparkling near one of the oak trees. I called to Grandfather to come and look at the beautiful lace I had found and he said it was the work of a spider that had woven it and the adornment of the morning dew that had enhanced it with sparkles.

"Treewalker, rain is Mother Nature's tears being poured out to thirsty ground that welcomes the contents fully. Each tear is caught, some below the surface nurturing future growth, and some remaining above on leaves and flower petals as gifts, sparkling in rays of light streaming through the oak trees."

Grandfather's words were gentle on my ears, and my heart soaked in each word like thirsty ground needing to be replenished. His tone was always soft and he wasted no words, yet he spoke more to me than I had ever known. He walked beside me, not in front or behind. His stride let me know what he was feeling and his words and eyes were always in harmony.

Grandfather Browndeer was a full Sioux Indian. His name was Hyacinth Browndeer: Hyacinth like the beautifully strong stalk of purple flowers that grew wild in the meadows near his home; Browndeer like the elegant creatures that graced those same wild spaces. I knew my grandmother's name was Winter Jasmine, but she was gone, now.

Grandfather wore a buckskin shirt that was shiny from years of wear and soft to the touch. His pants were worn through at the knees and covered in berry stains in shapes I often tried to see pictures in, like I did at home when I laid outside on the ground looking up at passing clouds. He had a knife that was tied to his hip with a leather band and it shined when the sunlight hit the hard, black stone. He used his knife for everything: digging in the ground, eating, or shaping objects from the branches and logs he found outside the cabin. His hair was gray and long and he wore it in a braid that danced on his back when we walked along. It came to rest on his waist when we sat cross-legged on the ground.

Grandfather's back always carried his eight-holed wooden flute tethered with a broad-beaded leather strap. He told me he carved his flute by the riverbed when he was a younger man. He wore a wide band across his forehead that had green and orange beading. He was always picking up tiny feathers along his way and he deposited them in the sides of the band: "Presents, Treewalker! The birds are sharing themselves and gifting us with the promise of new growth soon to come."

I had seen a basket of feathers near the cabin and had wondered about them. Grandfather never missed these feathers on our walks and bent down with respect to gather them and gently place them in the band. There seemed to be such importance to him when it came to gathering feathers and I wanted to know more about it, but I did not know if I should ask.

My grandfather loved to play his flute. He would inhale music and let it rattle around in his mouth until he had all the flavor and then exhale sounds that brought critters from every corner of the woods. Music filled the air with color, excitement, and blissful joy. We would sit until the long breath of what he tasted echoed its worth through the woods, only rising when it had been fully absorbed into all that was there. We walked without words, letting our feet continue the music that still filled our beings and let our hearts dance on the rest of the journey.

I liked walking alongside my grandfather. It gave me a sense of belonging. Grandfather said I was like a leaf on a tree, small, but a part of something larger, like he is to the Great Spirit. I felt peaceful with Grandfather and did not want to think of when I would not be with him. He must have felt my thoughts, for he spoke to my fear: "You will always be with me Treewalker. When a leaf falls from the tree, it is not forgotten, the leaf slips quietly into the ground and rests, waiting to rejoin the tree again because leaves come from the innermost part of the tree and bring forth the beauty that lies within. In your life, Treewalker, you will fall many times, just like the leaves fall, but you will never be forgotten or alone."

"But I have always felt alone, Grandfather. I feel more alone when I am with my family than I do when I am by myself."

"You feel alone because you do not have what you desire, Treewalker"

"Grandfather, what is it that I desire?"

"Child, you desire to stay on a tree that cannot help you be strong and filled with the nourishment that will bring growth to provide life for you. See that dead hollowed-out tree over there, the one that has very few leaves?"

"Yes, Grandfather."

"What is different about those leaves?"

"They are brown and falling off now, Grandfather. The leaves on trees around them are green and full and the branches are clinging tightly to them."

"That's right, child, this tree is dying of the sickness within it and it cannot offer anything to the tiny leaves it produced."

"Why can't it, Grandfather?"

"The tree's roots are too shallow and they are not drawing from the source of nourishment that runs deep within the ground. The only hope for the leaf to grow into the heart of a tree is for it to be blown beneath a healthy tree and join the deep roots that drink of the nourishment."

"Does the wind know where to blow the leaves and which trees will accept the leaves, Grandfather?"

"Yes, Treewalker, the wind is controlled by the Great Spirit. Some leaves do not stay under the trees of growth but are carried by gusts of wind and gather in piles and are swept away. You must not cling to a dying tree if you want to bloom and grow and know the fullness of your life. Seek to listen to the Spirit of the wind and allow it to guide you through the seasons that you fear the most, Little One. There are seasons of warmth and seasons of bitter cold, but without seasons there is no hope of growth. Rain can produce growth, but too much rain can create weariness, which leads to the death of hope. There is pain in the plowing and feeding of the soil that bears fruit."

Grandfather was silent for a short while, allowing me to think on his words. Then he asked, "You like the corn that comes from our garden Treewalker?"

"Yes, Grandfather."

"Without a little toil and some rain and feeding of the ground, it would not have grown and would not produce the sweet taste you like so much."

"But why must this happen, Grandfather? Why must there be so much pain needed to grow?"

"Without pain, we would not know we needed to grow, Treewalker."

I stood silently and thought of the pain I had known in my life and wondered if the rain from my tears had grown anything but fear in me. I did not know if I could make it through another season of the rains that pounded on me beneath my hollowed-out dead tree. I knew I did not want my first season of warmth from being with my Grandfather to ever end, but I knew it would. I had only one more question for Grandfather, "Was I blown here beneath your tree, Grandfather?"

He said nothing, but his dark wet eyes spoke the answer. I placed my tiny hand in his and felt tears hit my cheeks as I realized my hope for being held in the heart and mind of someone would come only as I allowed my tiny leaf to rest beneath the firmly planted tree of my Grandfather.

Chapter 3

Peace Pipe Lesson

Grandfather had a special pipe he kept in a wooden box in a corner of the cabin. He brought it out only once while I was there, inviting me to sit and partake of it with him. The pipe had a long shaft with purple and orange beading and a hollowed-out antler at the end held special leaves he lit by striking two rocks together. There was buckskin strapping cut very fine to hold large wooden beads and a deer hoof he had found by the edge of the stream we went to each morning. Feathers were carefully placed in tiny slits cut in the strapping, and a small leather pouch held the leaves he crushed between his hands and carefully placed in the pipe.

When he smoked, his cheeks would suck in hard to get the leaves to ignite. His face looked like the ground that he plowed, with deep furrows in his brow and sunken cheeks where only the bones were sticking out. Slowly, a little puff of white smoke would appear from the end of the pipe. I liked watching him as he moved easily and did everything without making it seem as though it was any work at all. He found pleasure in all that he did, his work, his steps, his words and life.

Grandfather could walk through the meadow without disturbing the grass, much like the gentle breeze that moved grass to the side and allowed it to come to rest back where it started. I tried to move as lightly as he, but my footsteps were heavy and I could always see where I had been. He made me a pair of moccasins that felt soft on my feet, but even then, when we walked together, I would look back over my shoulder and see only my footprints in the grass. I longed to know how he could walk so effortlessly and gently. He spoke once about not allowing my heart to be heavy and I wondered if that was why my footprints could always be seen and not his. I wanted to learn how to walk as Grandfather did and lighten the heaviness of my heart, but I was afraid the weight of it would break Grandfather's heart and I could not bear the thought of bringing him sadness.

"Treewalker, it is time." Grandfather always had a way of capturing my thoughts and depositing them back in the ground where I sat.

"Time for what, Grandfather?"

He handed me the pipe and I tried to do what I had watched him do, but I choked and felt the sting in my nose and throat when I inhaled. I coughed and handed the pipe back to him.

"You are not ready, my child, to inhale so deeply of this yet, but you will come to that place and learn to breathe deeply. I can breathe in deeply of the peace pipe because I have placed the heaviness and troubles of my heart into hands that are able to turn them into puffs of smoke. It brought peace to me and lightened my way. When the heavy burdens are released, one can breathe much deeper of all that is good. I see the desire in you, yet you are not ready because you are holding tightly to pain. The weight you carry covers you like your blanket. But you must not wrap yourself in the heaviness of it or you will never walk the path to freedom and peace."

I could not imagine being able to let go of all that was inside of me. I had wrapped myself tightly in my blanket of shame to keep everything in, yet being here with Grandfather in his warmth was beginning to tear holes in it. I thought of the first time I saw my grandfather's cabin and how the sunlight found the holes in the walls and drifted in. Now I wondered if Grandfather's words of peace were beginning to do the same to my heart's walls of fear and shame. I wanted his gentle passage through my heart, but it scared me to let him completely in to see all that was buried there.

I had a cemetery of tombstones within me that bore the names of all the evil actions that had occurred in my life. So many shameful things were buried there. I walked through that cemetery often, looking at each marker and remembering, letting the words on each stone tell me over and over again how unworthy I was of anything good in life. Each time my body and mind was violated with torturing attacks and cutting words, it dug another hole in my heart where I tried to bury it so deeply that I could forget. The memories wrote the words on the tombstones that created my

cemetery of shame and I read them as I walked alone in the nights.

I did not want anyone to discover what was buried there and

see all the badness within me. I knew what was written on the

tombstones in my heart of shame could cause my grandfather to go

away. My father chiseled that message deep on the stones every

time he told me, "If you let anyone know what happened, they will

never want to be around you."

I knew I would never be able to escape the cemetery that my

father's words had put into me, nor the weight of each stone marker

bearing the memories of his attacks. And I could not let

Grandfather find out about all my badness and risk him wanting to

leave me.

It did not matter that I had always tried to run away and

forget about that cemetery. No matter how high I climbed in a tree

or how fast I ran through the grass, my shame footprints were

always behind me and I always walked back knowing no other way.

Spending time with Grandfather was starting to give me a new

picture of what life could be outside the cemetery walls. I liked

what I saw and felt, as I viewed it through the tall iron gates of my own cemetery. But I did not believe I would ever be totally free to walk out and leave behind the shame I knew so well. I believed the world beyond my cemetery gates belonged to special children, pretty children, children whose parents loved them. It was only a dream for me, a dream from which I always awoke to find myself sitting on the cold familiar shame stones. I knew this time with Grandfather was just an extended, beautiful dream and I would wake up soon and be back in the nightmarish reality of my life.

I could not let Grandfather know about that life, for I had promised my mother that I would never tell and I could not risk her leaving me forever, just like I could not risk Grandfather leaving me. I loved being with him and seeing life through his eyes, even if it was for just a moment of time. I knew I could not let his words of light and peace go too deeply into my heart and uncover the dark secrets of my life.

"Where has your mind taken you, Treewalker?"

Grandfather's words startled me and I replied to him quickly, "Nowhere, Grandfather." But he looked at me as he had the day I first met him, and I knew I had answered him from my fear.

"Treewalker is that your truth?"

I stood up to run away, for that is how I always dealt with feelings of shame that came over me when I did not know how to answer from the truth. I did not know how to speak about the fear inside of me. Grandfather motioned to me with an outstretched hand to sit back down. It was not a suggestion; it was strong and intentional, yet also gentle and caring. I crossed my ankles and let my body slowly descend to a sitting position with my head buried deep between my knees and I folded my arms tightly around them. I struggled to breathe. I was trying to run from the words of my father and the sight of so many tombstones; I could not catch my breath.

"Look up, Child," Grandfather's voice was gentle.

I could not look up and allow Grandfather to see my truth, the truth I wore in my eyes. "No Grandfather, I can't."

"Child, look up. I feel the heaviness of your heart, I know how to release it and allow it to rise from you like the crushed leaves that went into my pipe rose as puffs of smoke to the sky. Let me take it in my heart's hands and allow the Great Spirit to set it free and refine it into something He will use."

"No, Grandfather, no one can use what is in my heart. It is all bad and you will choke. It will sting like the smoke from the pipe."

"You are a child and are not meant to inhale the bitterness and intensity of what you have been made to breathe. The Great Spirit has prepared me to take your painful heart and place it within His hands."

"No, Grandfather, I can't give this to you or anyone!"

"Treewalker, your heart can be set free by his peace if you let it. Look at me. Watch as the smoke rises to the light of the sky."

I wiped the tears from my eyes on the sleeve of my shirt and tilted my head to allow one eye to look up cautiously. I watched the smoke rise and open in small rings as he drew deep breaths and slowly released it. The puffs floated high between the branches of the trees and disappeared. I could feel my body begin to relax and my head rose up out of the protective pocket between my knees as I stretched my neck to follow the rings climbing higher in the sky. Just like the smoke that drifted up and away, I allowed my heavy thoughts to go with them. I sat a long time looking up at the sky, feeling the presence of my grandfather and wanting to release what was deep inside me, but just as I began to exhale, my fear stuffed the words and I remained silent. I felt the power of my shame bring the sky tumbling down upon me and take the breath of my words from me. I could not speak, only position myself back into the safety of my knees to hide my heart from Grandfather's eyes.

He sat beside me for the remainder of the long afternoon, not speaking or trying to free me from my protective shell, only breathing. His deep, relaxed breathing was captivating. I listened to him and my eyes grew heavy and my mind drifted into sleep.

When I woke up, Grandfather was still sitting beside me and bent over to whisper in my ear. "I planted daisies on each and every one of your grave sites and have replaced the words on the tombstones. You will learn to see both and your cemetery will become a garden to share with everyone."

I gazed at him in amazement. "How did you get there, Grandfather? How did you know?"

"It doesn't matter, Child, it isn't about knowing. It is about embracing the fear and allowing yourself to rise above the pain. This is how to accept the gifts of the Great Spirit."

I did not understand what Grandfather was saying, but I knew it was important. I tucked his words away in a protected pocket of my heart and took a deep breath of the air that seemed

filled with hope and kindness.

Peace Pipe

Chapter 4

Picture Day

One morning after we had eaten our biscuits, I went outside to draw pictures in the dirt. There was so little in that cabin that, when I closed my eyes, I could see everything quite clearly. There was no furniture; only two mats woven from grasses lay on the dirt floor and a fire stove made of rocks from the streambed. A wooden crate held a pot, two flat pans, two tin cups, one pronged utensil that Grandfather used to pull meat from the fire, and his peace pipe. The flour, lard and salt for his biscuits were stored in tin containers that sat on a shelf high up on the wall. He told me that the critters liked to visit his home and help themselves to what they found to

eat, so he kept everything they might like in the tins.

Grandfather kept the roots he dug from the ground stored in

a cellar in the side of the earth and I was always scared about

adventuring into that dark place. I had learned that going into any

place with only one way out was not safe for me. I did not like dark

and musty-smelling places; they reminded me of my father and the

places he took me to rob me of any sense of worth through his

violent, invasive actions. When Grandfather had to go into the

cellar, I always waited outside.

One day I found courage enough to place my head far enough

into the cellar to see brown burlap bags bulging with the roots he

had dug and potatoes that he had planted the summer before. A

large elk skin and two raccoon hides were strung up over some

leather strapping at the far end of the cellar. Large glass canning

jars with lids contained rice and beans that he had purchased from

the trading store he went to twice a year. He would exchange the

animal skins and trinkets he had made with his hands for the things

his ground could not produce. I never heard him talk about money,

other than the fact that he had none and never wished for any.

"Money gets in the way of life," he would say. "I choose to live life simply from what I have and not wish for more than that."

When something scurried out of the cellar, I jumped back.

"It's only a squirrel, Child, no need to be frightened." Grandfather's voice was calming, but I was still scared.

Rodents, especially mice, terrified me. Once, my father had held me down and dangled a large mouse over me, threatening to let it nibble my nose and face as he said my face wasn't worth anything as it was. I could feel the weight of his body on me and smell the stench of his sweat and the strong tobacco from the cigarettes he smoked and I could not breathe. I screamed and my mother came out and stood over me and laughed as she said, "it's only a little mouse!" At her words, I stopped screaming and stared at my mother's face, shivering in fear, pleading with my eyes for her to see how scared I was and protect me. She looked at my father and then turned and went back into the house.

My father got up and dropped the mouse onto my face. I screamed as I felt it crawl down my face and body and I turned over, curling into a tight, sobbing ball as I tried to escape the tingling, burying my face into the dirt. My father laughed as he said, "That's where you belong, in the dirt, where all trash ends up." I felt the pain in my heart penetrate my side as he kicked me hard with his heavy boot, flipping me over to stare into his dark eyes. My heart sunk into a deep hole as dark as his eyes. Words of shame echoed in my head, tangling with his cruel laughter. I wanted to cause my breathing to stop. I wanted to numb my body and never feel again. I closed my eyes and allowed my mind to give me a helper to carry the pain and intense feelings rushing through my five-year old body. I welcomed my helper and released the pain.

I jumped from the memories as Grandfather appeared out of the cellar, carrying something wrapped in large leaves. He placed it in my hands. It helped calm my racing thoughts and remove the pictures that played so vividly across my mind. "What is it, Grandfather"?

"Open it, Child."

I carefully removed each layer of leaves. Inside was a beautiful fan-shaped object made of feathers, small and large ones, and when I touched it my hands felt a softness I had never known. There were colors of grey and white and touches of blue and bright yellow woven from the variety of birds that lived in the woods and around the cabin.

"This is so beautiful, Grandfather," I breathed.

"Your grandmother made this, Treewalker. She carried it with her on the day we became one. She loved watching the birds in flight, but when she saw them gently land on the special windowsills of their world, she would have me sit with her and try to catch a glimpse of the picture they saw. Your grandmother smiled with her whole face when she was watching the birds." Grandfather smiled, then went on: "I asked her once if I brought such a smile to her face and she answered, 'You make my heart smile, but my face is for these fragile creatures that show me the way to rest and enjoy what the Great Spirit has made for me.'

Treewalker, I can still hear her words and feel her presence with me as I walk the paths. Each feather I pick up, I feel another touch of her heart on mine. I can feel her sitting by my side and see her heart smiling at me. I know that Grandmother would want you to have this now, my child. I do not need it as you do. I have the gifts of feathers along the paths. She has long been planted in my heart by her words and gentle actions. My desire is that when you use it, you will feel the gentleness of your grandmother's caring heart. I hope you will allow yourself to sit and view life from the windowsill she loved to sit at so often, the place where she found her peace."

I did not feel worthy to receive such a gift, yet I could not stop running my hand over the softness of that fan. It was seeping deep into my heart and mind and I felt my grandmother's love and caring and I could not hand it back to him. I wanted all that it stood for and I wanted to sit on the windowsill with my grandmother and see life as she saw it. I wanted to keep this precious gift, but I did not want it to be destroyed as most everything in my life had been. So I carefully wrapped it back in the leaves and asked Grandfather to keep it safe for me.

"I will, Child. And it will be here for you whenever you need her smiling heart to touch yours and soothe the burning pain that you feel so often from your windowsill on life. My heart smiled as I thought of Grandmother sitting with me on the windowsill, pointing out the different views that were just beyond my perception. I smiled as I felt her gentleness and peace, knowing she was smiling at me with her heart.

We walked back to the front of the cabin and I did not feel the ground beneath my feet, only the softness of the feathers and a lightness to my thoughts. I walked into the cabin and saw how the sunlight was making shadows on the walls, peeking in through the gaps between the logs. Some gaps were wider than others; I had learned how to position my mat away from the larger ones, away from the cold night breeze. My eyes drifted to the one thing that hung upon the walls of the cabin—a frayed blanket with tiny white blossoms woven on a dull red background.

"Grandfather, what is that?"

"Your grandmother's wedding blanket. She wore it around her shoulders every morning to fetch water for her tea." I listened as Grandfather remembered aloud how she had sat before the fire holding each of the thirteen children born to her, cradling them tightly near her heart. He always spoke more softly when talking about Grandmother and the children he brought into the world with her.

He took the blanket down from the wall and placed it around my shoulders. It was heavy and billowed around me like a teepee. I felt safe and grounded and special, like I did holding the fan she had made of feathers.

"This was the beginning of life for each of our children, Treewalker. Grandmother would wrap each child in her arms after I carefully took them from the birthing place. She would fold the blanket around her and the child and carry them with her on all of our journeys until they were strong enough to walk alone. I would hunt and bring the hides that she made into clothing to keep them warm. One by one, they left and found the shelters that they desired and Grandmother grieved for all of them and I comforted her with my flute."

I could not imagine anyone wanting to leave this place, the comfort of her arms (something I had never known in my own life) and the gentleness of my grandfather's words, which my starving heart was devouring. I found such a sense of safety and comfort with the wedding blanket wrapped around me. I did not want to ever remove it, but after a few moments, Grandfather took it off my shoulders and placed it back on the wall.

I felt sad and empty when he took it from around my shoulders and my eyes sunk to the floor thinking he had taken the warmth of my grandmother away from me.

"Treewalker, life cannot continue if we spend our time wrapped in a blanket. You enjoy the warmth of the blanket because you have known the chill of cold that life brings. You can come back to the blanket when you feel the chill, but you must not stay wrapped inside. Grandmother used her blanket to wrap others who needed warmth and safety. She wrapped herself only in it for the short walks to the stream and to remind herself that she had the comfort and safety that she needed.

She did not speak often, Treewalker, for her truth was spoken in the comfort she gave to all who were around her."

"I wish I would have met her, Grandfather."

"You have, Treewalker. You know her through all that you see around you and the feather gifts the birds leave in memory, and most of all in the comfort that she wraps around you in the sunlight that floods our cabin each day."

"Is that why you don't fix the holes in the cabin, Grandfather?"

"Yes child, I never want to shut the warmth and light from her eyes out of this place. It penetrates the chill that came over my heart when she left. I found my joy as I built my life around healing the sadness of her heart and seeing light come to her eyes as she walked with the Great Spirit. When she came to me from her family, her eyes were dark, much like yours are, Treewalker."

"I took pleasure in helping her uncover the treasures of her heart. One by one she laid the stones of her shame down from being called a half-breed by her family. Your Grandmother never knew that there was any other way to live than covered in shame. But I saw strength in her, Treewalker, a strength I had never seen in any other person. She walked with her head down but her heart's eyes open. All who approached her were met with hands reaching out to help.

"From the moment I came close, I knew that my heart would shelter her and find purpose in doing so. Through many days and years of walking the path together, she began replacing the stones of shame with the feathers she found as we sat watching from the birds' viewpoints. She taught me how to release what I wanted and accept what I needed.

"There was a time, Treewalker, when I wanted to prove to myself and all around me that I was strong. Being brave and being the best was all I thought about. I went on a hunt during the spring festival to prove to all within the camp that I was worthy of being part of the inner circle of young braves who were chosen for future leaders. It was during that Hunt that everything changed for me. I came upon a young cub that was alone and wandering, bellowing for its mother and I thought that if I stayed hidden, the mother would come back and I would have a chance to kill it and take it back with me to prove myself. I waited a long time and watched as the cub finally laid down in sorrow, believing all hope was gone. Something inside me changed. I allowed the pain and sorrow of that cub's grief to touch my heart. I was about to go to the cub when the mother returned. She licked her cub and gently put him in her mouth, carrying him with her. I allowed the moment of grief from this small cub and his mother's compassion to overtake my mind's seeking for self-satisfaction and proving myself.

"I went back to camp that night with nothing in my hand. They chanted that I was weak and a coward, but my heart had found peace and strength that I could not speak of to any there. I was banished to live outside of the camp. I discovered this clearing in the woods where I built the cabin and found my life without the approval of others.

"The day I laid down my bow, the Great Spirit gifted me with the ability to read hearts and feel deep pain of others. I am honored to be a guide to all that visit me here, Treewalker and I will walk with you so that you discover the gifts the Great Spirit has for you. In time, you will learn to put down what weighs so heavily on your heart and discover how to replace it with the feathers that are left for you along the path as Grandmother did. I will take great pleasure in walking the path with you and seeing the light that is within you find your eyes again."

I went outside to try to hold these words in my mind, to draw the cabin, Grandfather, Grandmother's wedding blanket, and all I had learned from him this day. I wished I had paper and pencil to capture it all and keep in my pocket so I could pull it out and look at it when I had to leave this place.

Grandfather saw the frustration on my face and stood beside me. "Treewalker, what bothers you?"

"I want to draw a picture, Grandfather, so I can always remember."

"Treewalker, draw the picture with your heart, then you will never forget."

"How do I do that, Grandfather?"

"Close your eyes and let your heart draw."

"I don't know what you mean, Grandfather."

"Do you remember when we sat on the rock in the stream?"

"Yes, Grandfather."

"Do you remember how you heard when you closed your eyes and ears?"

"Oh, yes, Grandfather."

"Draw your pictures in your heart the same way, Little One."

I closed my eyes and felt the warmth of my Grandfather's quiet voice, the safety in his presence, the softness of the meadow as I sat in its lap. I saw the way the trees framed the view of the stream that we walked to each morning and the sunlight painting new pictures on the walls of the cabin as it danced through the cracks. I painted all these pictures in my mind and showed them to Grandfather with the smile on my dirt-smudged face. I loved the pictures I had drawn and I carefully placed them in a special part of

my heart. These were pictures that I kept and looked at often when

I was alone and scared, without the gentle voice and eyes of

Grandfather to embrace me.

Chapter 5

Dream Catchers

I awoke to the smell of hickory smoke, which filled the small cabin that housed everything that was useful to Grandfather. He would say that he owned nothing, only needed a few things to tend to life. I stretched myself out and flattened the wrinkles that creased my shirt and pants, smoothing the wild strands of hair that I was certain popped out everywhere. I liked that Grandfather did not have any mirrors. The only time I saw my reflection was in the quiet part of the stream that laid still and rested on the pebbles. It was the place we drew fresh water to soothe our throats on those hot summer days.

When Grandfather looked at me, I never felt he looked at what I saw in the mirror. His eyes would grow wet and deep and gentle like the dark stones when the stream washed over them. I never wanted him to turn away, or even speak. I just stood soaking in all that I could of his eyes' warm embrace. He motioned for me to sit and I plopped myself down cross-legged on the dirt floor and eagerly put my hands out for the warm biscuit. We never talked when we were eating, but there was always something to share when we finished eating and took the cooking utensils to the stream to wash.

This day was no different, yet Grandfather's stride was quicker as we walked along. He said nothing until we reached the bank of the stream.

"Treewalker, your tears caught my net last night. "

I stood confused, not understanding. "My tears, Grandfather? When did I cry?"

"Your dreams came to my net when you were sleeping. Sit, I want to hear more of your heart."

"Grandfather, I don't know what my heart has to say." I knew that these words did not come from the truth, but Grandfather did not look at me as he usually did when he saw this in me.

He only spoke gently, "Treewalker, your heart speaks every night. I have heard the stories of your tears in the night. Your heart holds things that no heart should carry. It is time to place them in my hands." Grandfather motioned for me to come closer, but I was afraid of how it was making me feel. My stomach got nervous; the biscuits I had eaten were ready to come out. I could not look at him and my fear shouted to me to *run, run fast and far and don't look back*! I ran and Grandfather followed me with his eyes until I was out of sight and still I felt a part of his heart following me. I did not want to run, but I did not know what else to do. Grandfather wanted me to share what could bring the end to my being with him. It would tear away my hope of ever being with my mother again.

I climbed a big oak tree and my tears came flowing out. My heart felt such deep pain. I had tried so hard to keep the secrets in. How could my heart betray me in the night by letting Grandfather hear what was hidden there? His net was too precious to hold what would come out of the cemetery that was my life. I knew I was not important enough to share my pain with anyone. Why would he want what was in my heart? But at the same time, I was scared that I could not hold it all in any longer. I looked down, allowing my mind to go to a familiar thought that had not come since meeting Grandfather. I was high enough up in the tree that if I were to close my eyes and lean forward, I could take away all the thought, all the pain, and never be a burden to anyone ever again.

In the distance came the sound of Grandfather's flute. The music he was playing fell on my heart like tears falling from my eyes. It was slow and quiet and seemed to whisper. I curled up, hiding behind one of the tree's big branches to listen. A bird landed on a limb behind me and I turned to see. It was small with tiny white feathers and a hint of grey on both sides of its wings. I leaned toward it and it flew gently to a branch on the other side of the tree as if it were guiding me. I turned my body and moved, following it and when I looked down, I saw the brown deer that had led me to Grandfather's on that first day. It was looking up at me with its dark brown eyes. His eyes were questioning yet soft and I leaned back into a small pocket of the large limb I was sitting on and let his eyes hold me. The small bird that had led me around to this side of the tree sat quietly just above my shoulder. I was protected from below and above.

Sunlight passed through a cloud and streamed across my face, making me squint. More clouds drifted in and I watched them form pictures before me.

"Treewalker," Grandfather's voice floated up from where the deer had been standing earlier and I looked down to see his caring eyes searching for me through the sunlight. "What are the talking clouds telling you, Child?"

"Talking clouds, Grandfather?"

"Yes, child, they have come to you to give you help."

"Help? For me, Grandfather?"

"Yes, they have come to speak truth since your fears are strong and bending your mind to the wind of despair. Lean back, look up and let them speak what your heart needs to grow strong."

I sat back and the clouds began moving into one large pitcher that poured into what appeared to be small cups that floated in and around it. As one cup was filled, it drifted away and another took its place. Soon the clouds formed one large cloud and it became dark like night. Just as I felt the first drip of rain, the sunlight touched the outer edges of the cloud and moved through it. When the light hit the center of the cloud, it became white and took the form of a feather. The feather appeared to be captured by the wind, drifting slowly until it was directly above the tree where I sat. I could not take my eyes off of it and as quickly as it came, it dissolved into the light of the sky.

I did not know how to put what I felt into words. My heart understood what I saw and it began writing a new script for my life story that I would only later come to embrace. There were no words spoken about the message my heart received and Grandfather never asked me to share. I let what I felt sink deep inside of me, some I understood and the rest I left for later.

After a while, I knew I was ready to come down and walk beside Grandfather and give him what I could of the pieces of my life. We sat for the rest of the afternoon by the stream near the meadow. I did not guard my heart and we did not talk about what I had seen. He listened to the words I could not say as we sat looking at the movement of the stream until the sun drifted slowly over the hill and I felt him breathe a sigh so deep, so painful, that it made me move close to him.

"What is it Grandfather?"

"My net is filled, child, and still there is more.... How do you hold what you hold and not speak of it in the daylight?

I sat for a moment before saying, "I am frightened to speak of the truth of my heart, Grandfather."

He nodded and took my hand as we quietly walked back through the tall grass of the meadow. As we walked, we watched the light fade and create shadows through the trees. I glanced back and for the first time saw Grandfather's footsteps next to mine. I knew it meant he had taken the weight of my heart as his. When we approached the cabin, he put his hand on my shoulder and quietly whispered, "Child, my net has been woven larger now and I can catch your dreams of fear and tears again tonight." I looked at him and wanted to ask why he wanted to hold my fears, but as he took my hand in his, all I knew was I felt safe, protected, and something I never believed I would ever experience...loved.

Chapter 6

July 1958

Grandfather woke early this day, and his ceremonial chants that resonated through the walls of the cabin fell heavy on my heart. The sound of his chanting was different than I had ever heard or felt from him before. I did not understand the meaning of his deep groaning but felt its importance pierce my heart.

I was uncertain if I should get up and check on Grandfather or remain lying still as I had often done at my own home when I heard my mother's painful cries. I knew that to get up and go to my mother's side was to invite the pain to be diverted from my mother to me. So I sometimes laid silently without moving as I listened to the sounds coming from the paper-thin walls. Those walls held no secrets from those who lived within them. The fleshy, violent tone was one I knew intimately, from hearing my father's fists pound against my own face and body many times. I remembered the pain, but hearing the helpless cries of my mother caused me to put my own protective thoughts aside and run to help her. I would pull his arms away from her and as he turned towards me, his eyes always struck the first blow. I never felt anything after that.

I had learned to take the blows and withhold my tears, because the sound of my father's laughter when he saw me cry was more painful to me than any pain he could inflict with his hands. I did not want to allow him the satisfaction of seeing the fear and pain he brought to me. I knew that seeing it on my face gave him such pleasure and I would not bow to his evil greed. This was my only source of personal power and control and I would not let him take it from me. I felt all the pain but decided he would not see it any longer on my face.

My father's stature was small but the glare from his eyes made him seem gigantic to me. His eyes followed me whenever I entered the room, and the power they exerted over me took my breath away. They were a poison I had been forced to taste too often when I ran to protect my mother. I knew that each drink of his eyes and blow from his fists took away more of my life, but my mother was so much more important to me than protecting any life that was inside of me. I knew my only hope of survival was to numb what I felt, watch for the next volatile attack, and plan my escape.

I learned how to read the language of my father's breathing at the very early age of four when I was thrown against a wall for saying something when he was frustrated and demanded silence. I watched him from that moment on and never let myself relax or take my guard down around anyone. Play became an enemy because if I allowed myself to indulge in it, I would not be able to stand guard, which invited an ambush from my father.

Each time I stepped in to protect my mother, it reinforced to me that I had no value to her other than taking her pain. I desperately wanted to earn the right to my mother's love. My child's heart hoped that if I could take enough of her pain, I might be worthy to feel a morsel of her love.

Being here with Grandfather had given my heart a vacation from standing guard and protecting others. I did not feel the need to protect Grandfather until this morning, as I lay on my blanket listening to his groaning. My heart wanted to help him, but it also wanted to release the pain coming from the memories that had been stirred within me. I did not know how to freely express pain, as my grandfather did this morning. I only knew what my father's words and angry fists had told me: *I was not worthy to let my pain be seen or felt.*

I was so caught up in my own thoughts that I jumped in total panic when my grandfather stood over me and called my name. "Treewalker, get up, we must go."

I jumped up, startled, and followed him out the door. It took until we reached the meadow before I was present with him, able to let go of my thoughts of home. "Where are we going, Grandfather?"

"To the memory tree, to the tree where I have placed memories of your grandmother."

He said nothing more and his quickened steps and intentional body language let me know I needed to maintain silence and match my steps to his. I was nearly running to keep up, but it was important to me to follow in his stride. It took until we reached the outer part of the meadow before he slowed and I saw that he had carried a very large pack with him. We stood before a giant oak tree whose branches came down to embrace us as we approached.

Grandfather's face softened as he stood looking up between the branches. He reached into the leather pack, pulling out Grandmother's wedding blanket. He spread it out upon the ground and motioned for me to sit. When we had settled ourselves, he reached into the pack again and pulled out biscuits. He had wrapped them inside the skin of a rabbit he had captured through the skillful use of his bow and cured on the tree outside the cabin. When he placed the biscuits in my hand, I was surprised that they were still warm.

One lone biscuit sat resting on the hide of the rabbit at the outer edge of the blanket. When I finished eating mine, Grandfather saw me eyeing it and simply said, "Grandmother won't mind, Treewalker."

It was then that I knew the meaning of the morning's chanting, the sorrow, the deep expression of pain, my heaviness of heart. It was about the deepest part of caring and remembering someone. These were feelings I was unfamiliar with, but deep inside, I craved to experience. I wondered how one earned the right to be cared about, to be loved so deeply. What created such a strong feeling in my grandfather for my grandmother?

I felt the fear of being alone and without love rush through me. My heart wanted to leap out of my chest and run to the embrace of the great oak's limbs. I wanted Grandmother to wrap me in her outstretched arms. I wanted to know how to freely express my pain as Grandfather did. I only knew how to keep the screams of fear and loneliness that resided inside of me quiet and hidden. I had learned that others' pain was much more important than mine. I learned this from watching and protecting my mother. She was always crying and sad, or screaming about her pain of being unloved. But it was always me reaching out to comfort her. There was no room for my pain or my fears or feelings of abandonment. So I found my place by absorbing the ridicule, blame, and punishment others were not willing to accept. I found a sense of belonging by making my mother happy, and it seeped into my heart

and became my only source of acceptance. When I helped her feel

better, I felt that I deserved to breathe and smile and live. I watched

for my mother's pain or hurt and need for being loved and I catered

to it with every ounce of strength I had. I could not enjoy anything

or feel free to move about unless I knew my mother was safe and

happy. I drew my identity from how well I managed to encourage,

love and protect her. I believed that if I did enough, my mother

would love me and want me and possibly care about my safety. Just

a smile from her after I had given her some little trinket kept me

chained to the hope of being enough. I did not know how to move

about life without that chain and feared constantly it might be

broken, so I watched her every move and facial expression as a

soldier standing guard.

When my parents had dropped me off at the edge of

Grandfather's woods, I did not fear for myself. I feared for my

mother. Yet she said nothing when I was pushed out of the car door

and the paper sack that contained my only earthly possessions was

thrown out the window by her careless hands without a single

word. I had believed that my watchful care of her was important and held value, yet standing there with Grandfather, I remembered the pain and rejection I felt. She had thrown away my care, like garbage. No emotion, no hesitation and no sign of her holding me in her mind as Grandfather was doing this day for Grandmother.

Grandfather's groaning for the loss of his beloved this morning was a reminder that I had no one who grieved my loss, no one who treasured me, no one who saw me as a valued gift. I was merely a piece of garbage to be thrown away. I knew I would never be of value unless I could find a way to be good enough for someone to want to keep me.

Grandfather's voice brought me back to the blanket I was sitting on and he spoke words of remembrance of the day Grandmother became a part of him. She was the sharer of his peace, his resting place, the equal participant in all that was his to give to others. He celebrated and honored her on that day, in that place, and I was included in the most important day of my grandfather's memory life.

I put my head deep into my chest and felt the pain of my grandfather's loss, felt the pain of not knowing how to comfort him or bring his joy back. His pain was enmeshed with my own. I felt the touch of his leathery hand on my shoulder and when I looked at him, his face was wet with tears. He whispered, "To express one's pain is to honor who the Great Spirit has made us, and to feel pain keeps one's heart soft and approachable, and ready to be planted." We sat silent until the sun began to go to bed and then Grandfather rose and folded the blanket, putting it over his shoulder for the journey home.

I pondered his words as we silently walked back to the cabin. Express one's pain...? How could I ever do that without causing more pain to myself, and to others? I had no one who wanted to know the truth about my family's world. No one would believe me, no one could ever imagine the brutality and cruelty that my eyes had seen and body had experienced.

This was the first time I did not believe Grandfather's words. They were not true for me, I had no right to feel or express feelings. I was only here to give to others and take their pain. I broke away from Grandfather's stride and ran to a tree that I climbed with haste. I felt safe here, hidden among the branches and high above anyone's approach. I had often climbed trees at home when my father turned his rage on me. I would run for cover hoping to escape the beating.

Now, I was hiding from Grandfather's words. He wanted me to show my pain as he had done, but I was unworthy to do this. I did not trust that I would be safe, that anyone could hold the truth of my life. I felt paralyzed by fear. I could not think, I barely could breathe and my heart pounded inside of me. This was the first time I had felt so scared since coming to Grandfather's.

My pain overcame me and I sobbed into the arms of that tree. I was unable to hold the waves of loneliness that came crashing hard against my heart, breaking through all the barriers. My throat and stomach grew sore from my sobbing, and when my tears had ceased, I was too exhausted to move.

The sound of a gentle breeze entered my ears, but as I looked down, I saw not the wind but Grandfather and his flute. The melody he played whispered renewed strength and comfort to my heart. It was warm and gentle as summer and I was enticed to come down and embrace it. I stood silently in front of him and he rose from the ground and placed the music stick in my hands. This time, as we walked together to the cabin, my stride set the pace for the journey.

Chapter 7

South Meadow Jewels

Sunlight woke me early, slanting in on my closed eyes and warming my tight body. I lay under the scratchy blanket Grandfather had recovered from the food cellar carved into the side of the hill by his cabin. The blanket smelled of earth and potatoes and was heavy on my tiny body, yet the weight of it comforted me. Grandfather always rose early and traveled his distance to join with the Great Spirit and embrace him with joy for giving another day. I never joined him for this time; once I asked if I could go and he said that one day, he would show me the way to journey for myself.

77

Grandfather had been quieter since our time at the memory tree and his thoughts seemed distant. When he returned from his journey this morning, his step was quicker and his face brighter. The tone of his voice was warm and hugged my heart, "I have a gift for you, Treewalker."

"Me, Grandfather, a gift for me?"

He put his hand into the leather pouch he wore around his waist and pulled out a handful of black juicy fat berries, dropping them into my open hands. "This is not the gift, Treewalker, only the nourishment to get to the gift."

I was excited and put the whole handful of berries into my mouth. My cheeks puffed out and my lips turned blue from the juice that squirted out the sides. I felt the trickle of juice on my face and wiped it quickly with my hand as Grandfather smiled at me. "You look like a young brave going into war, Treewalker, with your blue streaks across your face."

I laughed, causing more of the juice to seep out of my overfilled cheeks.

"Can I see my surprise now, Grandfather?"

"Yes, Child, we can go now."

We walked in a new direction this morning, for the sun was on the right side of my face. I had learned from Grandfather that to go to the water in the morning, you feel the warmth on the left side of your face and to come home in the evening, it must be on the right side. He had taught me that the sun and moon give good directions and that I needed to watch them and listen to their guidance.

We walked a greater distance this morning and the handful of berries was not enough to keep my stomach from growling. I was used to being hungry from living in my family and I could make my feet keep walking when I was tired and weak. But the thought of a surprise for me this morning gave me added energy. Grandfather must have heard my stomach complaining, for he reached into his pack and pulled out a fat piece of deer jerky for me to gnaw on while we walked. It was salty and chewy and I liked how it lasted such a long time. When I finished the jerky, I was thirsty, and Grandfather handed me a small, flat, smooth stone to put in my mouth and soothe my thirst.

"We are almost there, Treewalker. It is just around the bend and I want you to close your eyes." He took my small hand in his and we walked the last piece together. I felt something deep inside

79

that brought a tear to my eyes. I felt special, safe and cared for. I never wanted to let go of this moment, this tenderness from such a leathered, rough hand. This was the first time that a hand reached out to me without hitting me, violating me, or tearing me away from something I wanted. This feeling is what I wanted, needed, desired so deeply but was so fearful of never having. Could I allow myself to feel so cared about, knowing it would be taken away when I no longer had Grandfather's hand, his safety, his gentle voice? Should I allow myself to embrace what I knew I would lose at the end of the summer? My fears interrupted the moment and it took Grandfather's words to bring me back to what he was giving me.

"We are here, Child. Keep your eyes closed and tell me what you feel and smell and sense."

I stood trying to push away the painful thoughts and fears, wanting to do what Grandfather asked of me.

"I don't feel, or smell, or sense anything, Grandfather."

"Let the clouds of fear and loss pass, Child. Take your time to hear the Great Spirit that walked with us to this place. He is here and He will always part the clouds like He parted the great waters for our ancestors. Keep your eyes closed and sit.

I sat down and crossed my legs, putting my chin into hands folded tightly to my body.

"Breathe, my child. Breathe deeply and let your chest rise and fall like the sun rises and sets on the hills over the water. Feel it push up the hills and fall gently into the waiting water. Listen for the gentle ripple it makes as it descends and waits for the call of its return."

I did as Grandfather asked and felt the rise and fall of my breath, allowing the movement of it to relax me and take away the cloud of fear that had invaded the joy of this day, this journey with Grandfather. I felt the softness of the grass and I began to smell something sweet.

"Where are we, Grandfather?"

"We are sitting on the edge of your surprise, Child. Embrace it with your heart and let it mend the worries of your mind. The Great Spirit led me here to gift you with this and help you find your space, your peace, and your joy. This surprise is for your heart and spirit. You cannot enter unless you let go of your fears and breathe deeply of what The Great Spirit has for you. When the memory clouds come, do not turn back, but sit awhile and breathe and let Him give you the peace that will drive away the clouds of fear."

My mind wanted to let go of the fear that was rising stronger inside of me and accept the gifts Grandfather had for me, but I did not know how. I knew how to accept pain, ridicule and abuse of my family but this gentleness and caring was unfamiliar. My role in life was to give to others and help make them feel good, but Grandfather did not need me to do this, he had the Great Spirit. I did not know how to receive and hold the gifts of caring and love that Grandfather wanted to give so freely. I only knew the familiar cemetery of shame. Its familiarity gave me a strange sense of comfort that I was afraid to release. How could I accept his gift and then have it taken away when my family came back and ripped it from my heart? I was confused and scared. I wanted to embrace all that Grandfather was offering me, but fear handcuffed me to the iron gates of shame. I wanted to be free to receive and experience all that these woods and Grandfather had been offering me. I wanted to be free to accept Grandfather's loving me.

The sun's warmth was a welcome interruption to my thoughts, allowing me to exhale the fears that my mind was dredging up from the dark corners of my life.

"It is time, Treewalker. Open your eyes."

"Oh Grandfather, it's beautiful!"

There was a soft, deep green meadow with white daisies and purple specks of color. Jasmine's fragrance tickled my nose. A crystal clear spring bubbled up over rocks, mirroring the color of the meadow and inviting me closer. I went to the edge of the water and bent down to take a drink. I giggled when I saw my reflection and the smudges of berry juice on both sides of my mouth and chin. Grandfather stood over me and I liked how tall and strong he appeared in the water's mirror.

"I could stay here forever, Grandfather. It is the most beautiful place I have ever known!"

"Open your heart's eyes and embrace this gift. This place has been planted in you. It is a place to run when you need to escape the fears and lies that come from the dark places of your life."

"But Grandfather, how could this be planted in me?"

"The Great Spirit has planted a beautiful garden for each of us to visit any time we desire. We only need to let go of our fear and allow him to bring us to the beautiful meadow He has created to comfort us. Your journey is in front of you and mine is almost passed. Look at the color of the jewels in this meadow. They are like your life, Treewalker—so beautiful. Don't let anyone or anything steal that beauty.

"The wind blew these colors here and many call them weeds, but they are strong and beautiful and bring joy to the hearts of those who visit and let the richness of color soothe their souls. I guided you here because the Great Spirit guided me to this treasure many years ago. I planted the Jasmine for your grandmother and we became one in this meadow. Today, Treewalker, my spirit became one with yours when I stood behind you at the water and cast my shadow onto yours. I allowed all that is good in me to join all that is good in you and we became one heart.

"I will be with you on all your journeys and nothing will turn me back. I am of the Great Spirit and He will keep me alive within you to walk with and talk with and listen to you. Your heart now beats in mine and my heart's hands hold yours to protect it and guide it with the gentleness your grandmother taught me.

"I pass the knowledge, beauty and peace of this place to you, my dear Treewalker. Find your way back as often as you can and bring your hurts to be planted in its ground. The seeds of each tear go deep within the fertile ground and produce the beauty you see before you. When your pain grows deep, come here and I will stand behind you near the stream. You will smell the sweetness of your grandmother and know that each tear is treasured and held in our hearts."

Chapter 8

The Gift

Grandfather did not know of the importance of this day to me, but it did not matter. He had a way of making all of my days special. Today was my seventh birthday, a day I looked forward to each year with unfulfilled hopes of it being recognized and celebrated. The closest I ever came to feeling that someone was celebrating my birthday with me was my sixth birthday when I was picking strawberries in the fields at the migrant camp. The sun was very hot that day and I was struggling to pick the ten crates of berries that my father insisted upon. I looked up to see a pickup truck pulling into the field in a cloud of dust. The driver was honking

his horn and the field boss yelled for us all to come over to where

the truck was now parked. I followed along behind the others,

wondering if we had done something wrong. I spotted several of the

men carrying watermelons and a large machete knife.

"We are going to celebrate today by having cold slices of

watermelon for everyone." *Could it be that they knew it was my*

birthday? I wanted to believe this was true and held it in my mind

as I sat down in a row of strawberry plants to savor the sweet, cool

taste. I needed so badly to believe that someone celebrated my life,

even if it wasn't true. I had always wanted to feel special, to be

recognized and held in the mind of someone without angry

thoughts. Those were the gifts I hoped for on my birthday.

I had been scratching lines in the dirt outside the cabin,

using a twig to keep track of the days I had been staying with

Grandfather. He had never asked me about this. He rarely asked me

any questions and this gave me a strong sense of safety and comfort.

Questions always led to fear that I would not say the right thing or

say too much. Grandfather seemed to know what I was thinking and

feeling without asking any questions. His understanding heart gave me freedom to relax from my watchful protection for my safety. He knew the path to my heart well and his gentle movement reassured me of his caring intentions. Grandfather never tried to rearrange anything within my heart but gave me new pictures to look at and choices that were mine alone to make. I was learning how to trust him, but the gift of his patient presence was frightening to me, too. Trusting in someone or something had only brought pain, wrapped in packages of Shame, Isolation, Unworthiness and Rejection.

Grandfather's presence in my life had been different. It was simple, gentle, and had no hidden messages. When I looked at him, I could see right through him into the woods, the meadow, the stream and the blue sky. He was a part of all that was good and beautiful about the woods and I felt him each time I sat and let my heart take in beauty. He had walked into my heart without me knowing it and was painting pictures on the walls that brought gifts of light and warmth and truth. He was never just Grandfather, he was the woods, the safety of the treetops, and the deer that guided me along the right path. I was learning to see clearer now, though I did not understand everything I saw. Grandfather let me put on the glasses through which he viewed life when we sat and talked by the stream or walked along the paths. He would swing me up to his shoulders and I loved catching glimpses of beauty from his perspective. I would sit tall and feel special. I had never sat on anyone's shoulders before; I would never trust my father's hands to lift me up to safe places—his hands only harmed. But I willingly put my hands out to Grandfather to lift me up.

Grandfather had taught me how to put my hands out and be lifted up above my view of the world. He had replaced my old overstuffed fear and shame-filled couch where I had always sat and viewed my life with a new one. It wasn't soft but it was gentle. It had no memories to it but I wanted to sit and relax on it and look out the window on all the sunlight touched.

My heart was discovering a new view on life. I was given a place to sit and rest and breathe when the war my parents brought to my life demolished all hope of love, happiness, and family. There was shelter in this resting place on Grandfather's shoulders, wearing his glasses, and I wanted to keep my eyes fixed only on this and not the raging storms. I knew what I wanted now but wasn't certain if I could keep myself sitting in this beautiful resting place without the strong shoulders of grandfather to hold me up.

His gentle voice interrupted my thoughts now, "Treewalker, are you not going to make your mark in the ground today?"

"No, Grandfather, I have enough marks now."

"Then we need to make our journey, Child."

I wanted to sit awhile with my thoughts, but his tone let me know it was time to go. As we walked, I asked Grandfather how he knew so much about the Great Spirit.

"I trust Him, Treewalker. He shows Himself in all that is around me. I walk with Him on the paths and He speaks to me as I let go of my questions and trust that He will provide. This gives me peace." He went on to explain that he believed that the Great Spirit knew what we needed before even we did and it was always waiting for us when we came to him with open hands and willing hearts.

"The Great Spirit speaks when we take the time to listen. That is how I knew to prepare for your coming to me Treewalker. He spoke to me and without questioning, I prepared to have you be a part of my life here. I did not need to understand, I just needed to trust what he spoke to my heart."

I stopped asking Grandfather questions and tried to listen for the Great Spirit. If it was true that He knew everything, then He should know it was my birthday. I needed Him to know and acknowledge my birthday if I was going to join my heart with the Great Spirit like Grandfather had and allow Him to hold all the parts of me.

Silently now, Grandfather and I walked along the meadow path our feet knew well. I spotted my favorite tree in the meadow and ran to it to climb but as I got closer, I saw that there were sparkles in the branches. Spiders had created lacey webs, and as I looked up, it seemed that there were jewels dripping down from every branch. Dewdrops captured the sunlight, reflecting rainbow colors and I could not take my eyes off the glittery beauty. I stood speechless, my mouth open wide in awe. I had a warm sense come over me, and my only thought was of the words my grandfather had spoken so often about the warmth of the Great Spirit. Closing my eyes, I felt His presence come over me and realized what I had been seeing. My heart whispered, *You do know it's my birthday and have left this present for me?*

My eyes felt damp but not from sadness. I was hearing the Great Spirit for the first time, not through Grandfather, but directly in my own ears and heart. He wanted to be *with* me! He knew what

I wanted most for my birthday and for my life. He wanted to be in everything about my life and love me. He cared about the smallest desires of my heart. He wanted to take my tears and set them dancing with rainbow colors through the bare branches of shattered dreams. He wanted to bring healing and refreshment to the dreams I held. As I stood listening, I felt as though Grandmother's wedding blanket was being placed around my shoulders, only this time, it was not heavy and it did not fall away when I opened my eyes.

I looked over at Grandfather as he sat silent along the path, and noticed that the rainbow of color I saw in the branches appeared to be sitting on his shoulders. When he saw me look at him, he stood up and the dampness I had only seen sit in his eyes now ran through the valleys of his cheeks. I ran to him and hugged his waist and there was no separation between us. We were one spirit, hearing the same voice and feeling the same warm breath of life.

I knew that what I received this day was a present I would spend the rest of my life unwrapping. I knew I needed to learn to close my eyes and ears to fear and shame and sit openhearted to the gentle whisper of the Great Spirit. His words would heal me.

Grandfather waited for me patiently to take the first steps to continue our journey on the path that day. He gave me complete freedom to continue on or return to the cabin. I stopped often throughout the day, examining everything with new eyes and discovering answers to my life that lay along the path, in the sky, and in the silence of my Grandfather, who walked beside me without pushing, pulling or influencing me in any way. I began to know the meaning of the talking clouds and the hollowed-out tree.

When we returned to the cabin at the end of the day, Grandfather turned to me and said, "Treewalker, you will learn much from the Great Spirit because you know how to be silent. Teaching your fears to do the same will be the challenge for you. But today you have taken an important step."

Chapter 9

Passageway

"This day we will finish our work at the stream, Treewalker." Grandfather was talking about the canoe he was making for me from a log that had drifted by one day when we were dancing with shadows in the meadow. The shadow dance is a dance of celebration of life that is within us. Grandfather explained he thought of it one day when he was a small boy and ever since, it has been an expression of his joy. I felt honored to have him share it with me, though he said he could not teach me, because it came from inside a person and not from the mind of a person.

Grandfather was always saying what we feel teaches us so much more then what we think. He was always saying to me, "Treewalker, stop thinking and feel the presence of all that is around you." I would try and there were times I did this in the meadow with Grandfather, but I was afraid of what I felt all of my life. I did not want to take in what I knew of life before coming to see Grandfather, because it brought too much pain and fear. I had created others inside me to feel and take these things in. I called them my helpers, but they had been very silent during the weeks with my grandfather. I had not needed them.

I picked up the flute and the hatchet and we took intentional strides to the stream. I loved holding the music tube and I tried to imitate the sounds that Grandfather made when he held it. I glanced now at Grandfather's hands, brown and creased as the pouch of leather he wore around his waist.

When we arrived at the stream, I sat quietly, watching him cut deep gouges into the log and shape it into our special canoe. There was so much force and power in those hands as he drew the blade back and plunged it deeply into the wood. I had only seen his hands while he was playing the music tube or braiding my hair or baking biscuits or planting the seeds for the garden.

Those hands calmed me as no hands had before. Even in the force he was using now, I felt safe. I loved watching him create; he used his leathered hands as skillfully as anyone I had ever known.

He worked quickly and almost like magic, chiseled two seats.

"Can we go for our ride, Grandfather?"

He looked up and motioned for me to come and sit inside, but he did not stop his work. I sat watching as he carefully smoothed the sides, the sharp blade held at just the right angle. He stopped only for a second to run the blade over a smooth rock to sharpen it. The sounds of his work were the music of creativity and I wished I could play it on the music tube. He took pleasure in every movement and joy flowed out of him like the beads of sweat that sat in the furrows of his brow. His mouth did not smile, it didn't need to, for I felt his joy in ways that I could not express in words. I was more alive sitting in that hollowed-out log than at any other time in my childhood. I was safe, I was watching joy play out, I was in the presence of the meaning of life and toil and I wanted to dance with the shadows.

The sun began to settle down to its nest behind the hillside before Grandfather put his hatchet down and said, "It is finished." He slid out of the canoe and into the water, gently guiding me around the marsh and out into the stream.

"Grandfather, aren't you getting in?"

"No, Treewalker. This is the ceremonial first ride for you."

I felt uncomfortable being held in the security of the canoe when Grandfather was in the cold stream. I did not know what being important was or what it looked like, but this felt important and yet it brought a sense of discomfort. He sensed my thoughts and walked around to the back of the canoe where I sat. "Close your eyes and make a memory, Treewalker. You will need this to navigate your life. Listen to your heart and not the voices of your fears. We are finished and our work is good and now you will need to complete what you are called to do."

I did not know what Grandfather's words meant, but I felt a sadness come over me. A chill pierced my heart and I sensed change was coming. When he pulled me to the edge of the stream, I looked up and the sky was red like it was on fire. Grandfather took my hand and I felt its warmth ignite my heart. I felt connected with

what was above and what was in my hand and they were one.

When I awoke the next morning, Grandfather was not there.

There was no smell of biscuits, no calmness, no sunlight dancing

outside on the ground. Only a heavy feeling of sadness and fear

whispered. The sound of a car came close and I did not rush to see,

because a familiar fear spiraled in my stomach and told me who it

was. My father and mother were back and Grandfather was

nowhere to be found.

I ran to the meadow as quickly as I could. Just as I got to the

stream, I saw the only person who had ever loved me round the

bend of the stream without looking back. I felt my heart grow cold,

and as I knelt on the wet stones, I heard the music tube grieving and

calling my name. Looking down, I saw the tears of my grandfather

in the wet stones and his words echoed in the emptiness of my

heart: *I will never leave you.* Yet he was leaving me and my heart

was breaking, knowing I would never see him again. I looked

toward the riverbank and there lay a feather, pure white and

glistening from the sun that hit its edges. I ran to pick it up and felt

the softness as my fingers passed over it with gentle thoughts of

Grandmother's touch that I only knew through the gifts of feathers.
My tears streamed down my face, sobbing the words "come back
Grandfather." The wind whispered through the trees and I could
hear his voice gently say, " as long as there is wind and trees and
streams to sit beside, I will be with you Treewalker". I felt his
presence as the breeze passed over my wet cheeks and kissed them
gently.

My heart did not want to leave this place by the stream, the
meadow's lush, green grass and white daisies, the paths that led
Grandfather and me to the memory tree and my special gift at the
South Meadow. I had discovered life outside of the tombstones of
shame. I had learned to breathe in peace and exhale fear. I did not
know if I could do this with my family around and without
Grandfather to help me.

There was a piece of me that had melted into him and knew I
would never be the same. He had given me all the best of himself.
He had given me a new view on life, love, peace and joy. He had
taught my eyes to see the passageway to truth and the freedom it
brought as I learned to travel on it. I had learned to listen to the
Great Spirit in the presence of my Grandfather. He had given me

hope and I would need all the strength of the Great Spirit to face my life with my family again. I tucked the feather into my pocket, running my fingers over it often as I made my way back to the cabin. This summer's vacation from fear and shame had given me courage to believe that I was important to someone. The sound of my mother's voice came crashing through the woods, disrupting the silence I had grown to love. I did not want the harshness of my family to violate this sacred ground. So I ran to the car just to silence the intrusion and as we drove away from the cabin, my hand tightly clutched to the feather hidden away in my pocket. I closed my eyes and my heart whispered; *I will never forget you, Grandfather Browndeer.*

www.treewalkersgift.com